EXCITING OUTDOOR CAREERS

MARINE BIOLOGIST

DWAYNE HICKS

PowerKiDS press

Published in 2026 by The Rosen Publishing Group, Inc.
2544 Clinton Street, Buffalo, NY 14224

First Edition

Editor: Greg Roza
Book Design: Rachel Rising

Photo Credits: Cover, JGA/Shutterstock.com; Cover, pp. 1, 3–24 Iurii Vlasenko/Shutterstock.com; Cover, pp. 1, 3–24 klyaksun/Shutterstock.com; p. 4 Aleksandr Merkushev/Shutterstock.com; p. 5 Magic Orb Studio/Shutterstock.com; p. 6 Ajm_a_l66/Shutterstock.com; p. 7 Hector Pertuz/Shutterstock.com; p. 9 Nomad_Soul/Shutterstock.com; p. 11 Verin/Shutterstock.com; p. 12 James Kirkikis/Shutterstock.com; p. 13 belizar/Shutterstock.com; p. 15 rospoint/Shutterstock.com; p.17 Dominic Gentilcore PhD/Shutterstock.com; p. 18 How Silent the Spring. Photograph. Retrieved from the Library of Congress, <www.loc.gov/item/93506538/>.; p. 19 Jacques Cousteau, peering out a two-man underwater observation chamber on board the "Calypso," as it docks in New York City for the International Oceanographic Congress. Photograph. Retrieved from the Library of Congress, <www.loc.gov/item/97519557/>.; p. 20 Riderfoot/Shutterstock.com; p. 21 Francisco J Ramos Gallego/Shutterstock.com.

Cataloging-in-Publication Data

Names: Hicks, Dwayne.
Title: Marine biologist / Dwayne Hicks.
Description: Buffalo, New York : PowerKids Press, 2026. | Series: Exciting outdoor careers | Includes glossary and index.
Identifiers: ISBN 9781499457216 (pbk.) | ISBN 9781499457223 (library bound) | ISBN 9781499457230 (ebook)
Subjects: LCSH: Marine biologists–Juvenile literature. | Aquatic biology–Vocational guidance–Juvenile literature. | Marine sciences–Vocational guidance–Juvenile literature.
Classification: LCC QH91.45 H54 2026 | DDC 578.77023-dc23

Manufactured in China

CPSIA Compliance Information: Batch #QWPK26. For Further Information contact Rosen Publishing at 1-800-237-9932.

CONTENTS

LET'S DIVE IN!

Some people just can't get enough of swimming, boating, diving, fishing, and other marine activities. As long as it's near, on, or in the water, they're happy as a clam! Some people turn this interest into a career. That's what marine biologists do.

Marine biologists study marine life. That includes fish, whales, sharks, dolphins, **plankton**, seaweed, and a lot more. They keep records on animal populations. They study marine **habitats**. They also study the affects that the actions of people have on marine wildlife. They work on boats, **submarines**, and on shore lines. They also work in laboratories and offices.

This marine biologist is using diving gear to study a coral reef and it's wildlife in Malaysia.

WHAT ARE BIOLOGISTS?

Biologists are scientists who study living things. This includes the structure and function of body parts, behaviors, animal groups, and wildlife interactions. They also study evolution, or the way animals change over time. Biologists often spend a lot of time in laboratories, but some, such as marine biologists, get more time in the field.

There are many kinds of marine biologists and they do many kinds of jobs. Like all biologists, marine biologists specialize in a specific area, such as marine mammals, invertebrates (animals that don't have a backbone), **algae** (shown at left), and so on. Some are specialists in several areas.

OUTDOOR ADVICE

Like other types of scientists, some marine biologists write papers and publish their findings in science journals, which can be a lot of work.

For many biologists, a day at work likely includes laboratory work, writing reports, and meeting with other scientists.

COLLEGE AND TRAINING

Most people who work as marine biologists have a bachelor's degree, or a four-year degree. Some continue on in school to earn a master's degree, which takes about five to six years. That degree could be in marine biology, biology, zoology, ecology, and even botany, the study of plants. Additional coursework will include mathematics, chemistry, and physics.

Marine biologists can improve their chances of getting hired by receiving training in related areas. A boating course will teach you to pilot and maintain a boat. A diving course will prepare you for a wider selection of jobs. First aid and **CPR** training also helps.

OUTDOOR ADVICE

Marine biologists sometimes have other professional titles. These include zoologist, fish and wildlife biologist, **conservation** biologist, and others.

Someone trained in scuba diving can help train coworkers. That makes them more attractive to employers.

GOVERNMENT WORK

Government **agencies** hire many marine biologists. The National Oceanic and Atmospheric Administration (NOAA) is a U.S. scientific organization that forecasts weather and keeps a close watch on Earth's oceans. The Food and Drug Administration (FDA) is a government agency that hires marine biologists to help create new drugs, keep marine food sources safe, and more.

The Peace Corps is a U.S. government program that trains **volunteers** in skills they can use to help people in developing countries. They help build schools, set up farms, teach about health care, and much more. The Peace Corps hires marine biologists as teachers and for leadership in the field.

OUTDOOR ADVICE

The National Marine Fisheries Service is a part of NOAA. They hire marine biologists to watch over fish populations and make sure marine food sources are safe. Some work on ships to make sure companies follow proper fishing practices.

Marine biologists also work for state fisheries and fish and wildlife conservation groups.

PRIVATE BUSINESSES

Government agencies are the largest employers of marine biologists, but private research companies also hire them. Environmental consulting organizations provide advice to both government and private groups. They make sure groups follow U.S. laws and conservation practices. Private research companies hire marine biologists to find new ways of making products from marine plants and animals.

Some marine biologists work in aquariums, zoos, and museums. They help care for marine wildlife and make sure laws are being followed. They may also lead educational shows. Still other marine biologists become teachers in high schools and colleges.

A marine biologist trains two harbor seals to do tricks at a zoo in Hungary.

PROBLEM SOLVERS

No matter where they work, a large part of a marine biologist's job is to solve problems. Marine biologists look for ways to stop the **destruction** of marine habitats. Many monitor or manage projects that could affect Earth's oceans. Species can be in danger when construction companies bypass safety and conservation laws.

Many of Earth's marine species are at risk due to water pollution. Much of this is caused by factories and farms. In recent years, very fine pieces of plastic called microplastics have been found in the bodies of marine species. Marine biologists are currently working to find a solution to this widespread problem.

OUTDOOR ADVICE

Marine biologists search for, monitor, and help reduce invasive species. This is a species flourishing in a habitat it's not meant to be in, resulting in damage to the marine habitat and its local wildlife.

This marine biologist is studying an algae bloom. This happens when algae takes over an area of water, which is unsafe for both wildlife and people. It is often caused by **fertilizer** runoff from nearby farms.

SUSTAINABILITY AND RESPONSIBILITY

Marine biologists work to protect marine habitats and species so they will be around for generations to come. The word "sustainable" is used to describe conservation efforts intended to protect the environment from future problems. For example, sustainable shipping deals with the methods used for shipping cargo that avoid harming the environment. This could mean developing new ship **technology**, redrawing shipping lanes, or limiting the amount of ship traffic in an area.

OUTDOOR ADVICE

Ecotourism is a sustainable approach to travel and vacations. Ecotourism companies provide tours that highlight conservation and natural beauty. Marine biologists help plan responsible ecotours, select areas to visit, and monitor the interaction between people and the environment.

Many marine biologists consider their efforts to help the environment their responsibility. They use their thorough training to help improve the world and keep our oceans safe.

Ecotours can be relaxing and beautiful, but they are also a chance to learn about the environment and conservation.

FAMOUS MARINE BIOLOGISTS

Rachel Carson was a marine biologist who worked for the U.S. Bureau of Fisheries. She was also a great writer. Her book *Silent Spring* introduced the general public to Carson's findings on pollution and its affect on people and wildlife. Carson's work helped show that conservation is everyone's responsibility.

Silent Spring addresses the harm farm **pesticides** do to the environment. By raising awareness, Carson's efforts eventually led to the creation of the U.S. Environmental Protection Agency (EPA).

Jacques Cousteau was not a trained scientist, but his name is now synonymous with underwater exploration. He was a skilled diver and photographer. He invented important diving technology, including the Aqua-Lung (scuba tank). Cousteau's numerous books and films helped shape the public's knowledge of Earth's seas and the wildlife in them.

YOU CAN DO IT!

Marine biologists need a lot of training before they can land a job. However, all that training pays off: the average pay for marine biologists in the United States is about $65,000. In time, marine biologists may earn more than $100,000. Government jobs pay well, and federal jobs usually pay more than state and local governments.

Can you see yourself on the deck of a ship mapping the ocean floor for NOAA? Or maybe as part of a team studying a newly discovered species of ocean algae? If so you might make a great marine biologist!

Marine biologists remind us how important Earth's seas and the life in them are to human beings.

GLOSSARY

agency: A government department that's responsible for a certain activity or area.

algae: Simple plants with no leaves or stem that grow near or in water. The singular form is "alga."

conservation: Efforts to care for the natural world.

CPR: A procedure used to restore normal breathing when the heart stops beating. Short for cardiopulmonary resuscitation.

destruction: The act of causing so much damage, or harm, to something that it can't be fixed or no longer exists.

fertilizer: Something added to the soil to help plants grow.

habitat: The natural home for plants, animals, and other living things.

pesticide: A poison used to kill pests.

plankton: A tiny plant or animal that floats in the ocean.

submarine: A ship capable of functioning underwater.

technology: A method that uses science to solve problems and the tools used to solve those problems.

volunteer: Someone who does something because they want to help and not for money.

FOR MORE INFORMATION

BOOKS

Hestermann, Bethanie, and Josh Hestermann. *The Fascinating Ocean Book for Kids: 500 Incredible Facts!* New York, NY: Callisto Kids, 2021.

Quick, Megan. *Marine Biologist*. Buffalo, NY: Scientific American Educational Publishing, 2025.

WEBSITES

Jacques Cousteau Facts for Kids
kids.kiddle.co/Jacques_Cousteau
Read more about the life and contributions of Jacques Cousteau.

Rachel Carson
www.ducksters.com/biography/scientists/rachel_carson.php
Learn more about the fascinating life and career of Rachel Carson, and find links to other inspiring scientists.

Publisher's note to educators and parents: Our editors have carefully reviewed these websites to ensure that they are suitable for students. Many websites change frequently, however, and we cannot guarantee that a site's future contents will continue to meet our high standards of quality and educational value. Be advised that students should be closely supervised whenever they access the internet.

INDEX